Just Like Arnold Lobel

by Melissa Erdman
illustrated by Chris Schafer

Harcourt
SCHOOL PUBLISHERS

p.7, p.11, p.13, ©Association for Library Services for Children, American Library Association.

Printed in China

ISBN 10:   0-15-377356-1
ISBN 13:   978-0-15-377356-3

Ordering Options
ISBN 10:   0-15-377148-8 (Grade 4 Collection)
ISBN 13:   978-0-15-377148-4 (Grade 4 Collection)
ISBN 10:   0-15-377843-1 (package of 5)
ISBN 13:   978-0-15-377843-8 (package of 5)

2 3 4 5 6 7 8 9 10 0940 17 16 15 14 13 12 11 10 09

You could say that Arnold Lobel was a born storyteller. When he was in second grade, he would tell entertaining stories to his classmates. Later, as an adult, Arnold would become an award–winning children's book author and illustrator. In fact, he eventually wrote or illustrated over seventy books for children.

Today both children and adults enjoy Arnold's special stories and characters. You may have read his delightful *Frog and Toad* books. Perhaps you have read his funny book called *Ming Lo Moves the Mountain*. If you have read any of his works, you know that Arnold Lobel was a wonderful storyteller.

Arnold was born in Los Angeles, California, on May 22, 1933. Arnold's parents had grown up in Schenectady, New York. After his parents got married, they moved to California. They lived there for about two years. The family moved back to Schenectady when Arnold was about six months old.

Arnold described himself as a "screaming, red–faced, ill–tempered" baby. Arnold lived in a large house in Schenectady. The home also had a nice front lawn. The streets there were lined with pretty trees. In his early years of childhood, Arnold was happy.

Later in his childhood, though, Arnold became sick. He had several illnesses. He was forced to stay in a hospital for weeks at a time. The hospital was right across the street from Arnold's school. Sometimes Arnold would look out his hospital window at the school playground. He would watch his classmates running around, talking to one another, and having fun. Arnold felt sad that he couldn't be with his friends and classmates. He could not participate in school for long periods of time, so he began to feel isolated, or apart, from other children.

Life became much better for Arnold when he reached middle school and high school. Arnold's illnesses began to go away as he grew older. He started to feel healthy again. He also learned something very important about himself at this time: he wanted to be an artist.

After high school, Arnold went to the Pratt Institute in Brooklyn, New York. Pratt Institute is one of the most famous art schools in the United States. Arnold enjoyed his time at Pratt. While there, he decided that he would like to be a book illustrator. A book illustrator is the person who makes the drawings or paintings for picture books.

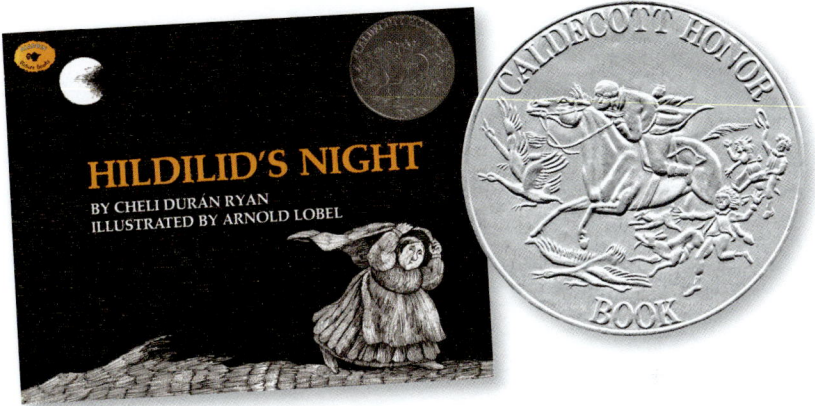

Arnold met a fellow student at Pratt named Anita. Anita also studied art. Arnold graduated in 1955. He and Anita got married shortly after that. They lived in an apartment in Brooklyn and later had two children. The children were named Adrianne and Adam.

In 1961, Arnold got a job illustrating his first children's book. The book was *Red Tag Comes Back* by Fred Phleger. Arnold's career as an illustrator had begun! During his career, he illustrated over sixty books by different authors. One of those books was Cheli Duran Ryan's book *Hildilid's Night*. This book was named a Caldecott Honor Book in 1972. This honor is given to an illustrator of children's books.

Arnold said that illustrating other people's books was "something different and challenging." Arnold did not make the same kinds of drawings for each book he illustrated. Instead, he used a wide variety of illustration methods. Some books were illustrated in pencil. These books had only two or three different colors. Some books were illustrated with just a black pen. Other books were illustrated in full color.

He made beautiful, accurate illustrations of dinosaurs for Peggy Parish's book *Dinosaur Time*. He made scary drawings for *Nightmares: Poems to Trouble Your Sleep*, by Jack Prelutsky.

Arnold illustrated a book that he wrote himself in 1962. The book was called *A Zoo for Mister Muster*. In the book, Mister Muster is a friendly man who loves to visit the animals at the zoo. Later in the story, the animals leave the zoo. They go to visit Mister Muster in his apartment. The police come to take the exotic animals back to the zoo, so the animals hide. The elephant hides under Mister Muster's bed. The monkeys hide in his sink.

The next year, Arnold wrote a sequel to the story called *Holiday for Mister Muster*. A sequel is another book about the same characters. In this book, Mister Muster takes sick animals to the seashore so they can get better.

Arnold Lobel once said, "I know how to draw pictures. With writing, I don't really know what I'm doing." Based on the books he wrote, it certainly *seems* like he knew what he was doing.

In 1970, Arnold published one of his most famous books. It was called *Frog and Toad Are Friends.* The book's main characters are a calm frog and a temperamental toad. They are good friends who spend a lot of time together. The book has five stories about Frog and Toad.

Arnold went on to write three more Frog and Toad books: *Frog and Toad Together, Frog and Toad All Year,* and *Days with Frog and Toad. Frog and Toad Together* was voted a Newbery Honor Book in 1973. This is an honor given for one of the best children's book of the year.

Most of Arnold's books have unique characters and a lot of humor. In his book *Owl at Home*, the main character, Owl, does some silly things. When Owl lays in bed, he sees two strange bumps underneath the blankets and gets worried. Owl doesn't realize that the bumps are his own legs and feet! There is a story in *Frog and Toad Together* in which Frog and Toad bake a delicious batch of cookies. They try to have "willpower" and not eat so many of the cookies. By the end, though, they have eaten them all!

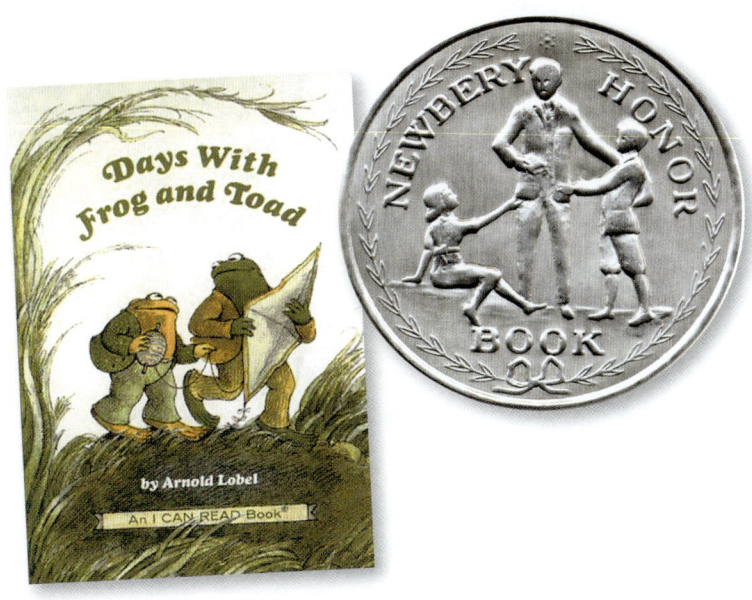

Arnold once said that he got most of his ideas for books from his own childhood experiences. Many of the characters in his books are childlike. For example, in the book *Small Pig*, the pig looks like an adult pig but acts like a child. Arnold's book *Giant John* is about a young man who becomes famous. Like a child, though, he is devoted to his mother. Mister Muster has a childish love of animals, even though he is a man.

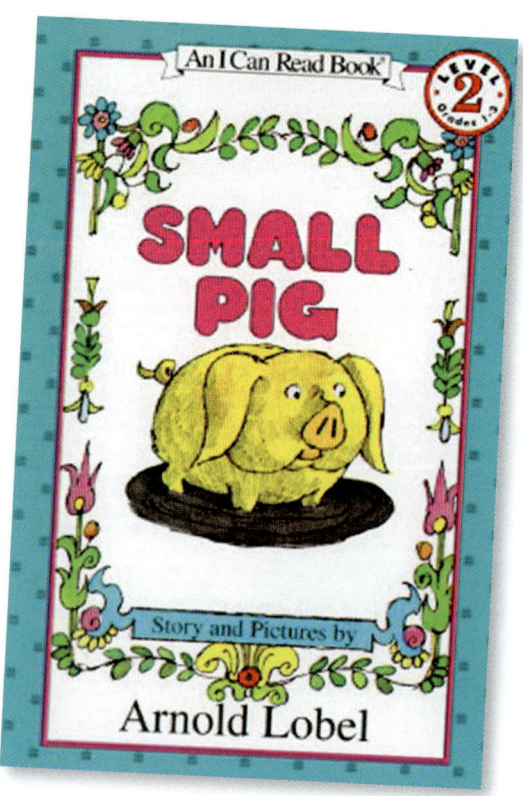

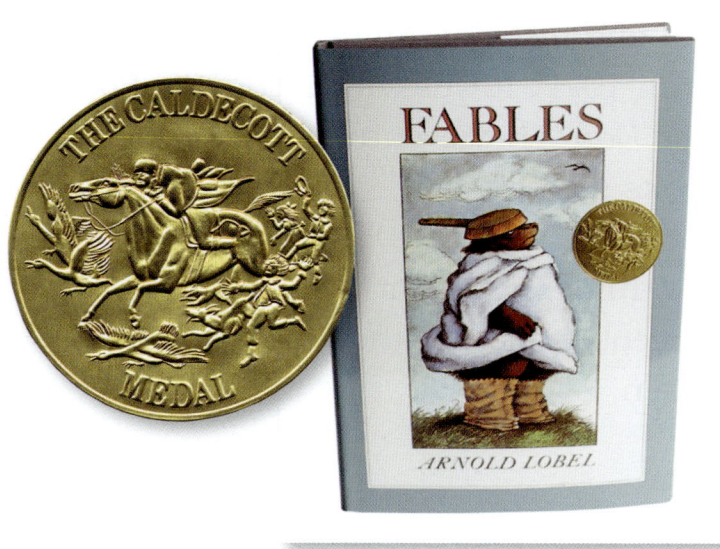

Arnold won the Caldecott Medal for his brilliant book titled *Fables*. Each of the brief tales in the book has a moral. A moral is a message that teaches a lesson. In one of the stories, a teacher visits the parents of a mischievous student. The teacher sees that the parents are just as silly as the child!

Another one of Arnold's books is called *Uncle Elephant*. In this story, a young elephant spends time with one of his elderly ancestors. In *Lucille*, a farmer's wife tries to make her horse, Lucille, prettier and more graceful. At the end of the story, the plan fails. Lucille, though, realizes that she is happy to just be herself.

Arnold and his wife, Anita, created a book together in 1977. It was called *How the Rooster Saved the Day*. They eventually wrote three more books together.

Arnold Lobel died in 1987. He once said, "I cannot think of any work that could be more agreeable and fun than making books for children."

Think Critically

1. List one fact and one opinion stated in this book.

2. What is a word that means almost the same thing as *ancestors* does on page 13?

3. What details does the author give about Arnold Lobel's childhood?

4. When did Arnold Lobel realize he wanted to be an artist?

5. How do you feel about Arnold Lobel after reading this book?

 **Art**

Be an Illustrator Study the illustrations in some of Arnold Lobel's books. Select one of the illustrations and sketch it. Try to make your illustration look like Arnold Lobel's.

School-Home Connection Share this book with a family member. Then go to the library and look for some of Arnold Lobel's books together.

Word Count: 1,214